Looking after Rabbits

Fiona Patchett

Designed by Kate Rimmer

Edited by Simon Tudhope

Illustrations by Christyan Fox

Consultants: Rabbit Welfare Association and Fund

Usborne Quicklinks

For links to carefully chosen websites where you can find out more about rabbits go to the Usborne Quicklinks website at www.usborne-quicklinks.com and enter the keywords **"pet guides rabbits"**

There you'll find links to websites where you can:

- Discover the right pet for you
- Watch video clips of how to care for rabbits
- Solve quizzes and find fun things to make and do
- Find fascinating facts about rabbits

Usborne Publishing is not responsible for the content of external websites. We recommend that young children are supervised while on the internet and follow the safety guidelines displayed on the Quicklinks Website.

Contents

All about rabbits

Rabbits are quiet, friendly animals. They might be nervous around you at first, but this guide shows you how to make them feel at home.

Two rabbits settle in faster than one rabbit on its own.

Friends forever

Rabbits are happiest when they have other rabbits for company, so it's best to keep them in pairs.

There are lots of different rabbits. Some grow big, others stay small.

This little rabbit weighs the same as a bag of sugar.

When choosing one, ask how big it will get. That way you can buy the right-sized hutch.

Wild rabbits

Pet rabbits are related to wild rabbits that live in the country. They all belong to a family of animals that includes hares and pikas. Hares and pikas are not kept as pets.

Hares are bigger than rabbits, with longer ears and stronger legs. They can run very fast.

Pikas are smaller than rabbits. They live in North America and Asia.

Types of fur

Different breeds of rabbits have different sorts of fur. Some have very long fur that needs brushing every day. Others have shorter fur that needs brushing once a week.

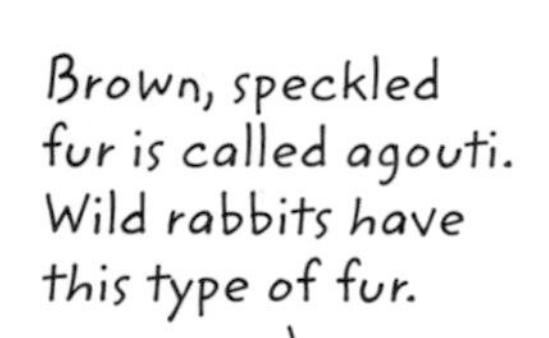

Brown, speckled fur is called agouti. Wild rabbits have this type of fur.

Fur that is 2-3cm (1in) long is called normal fur. This Blue Dutch rabbit has normal fur.

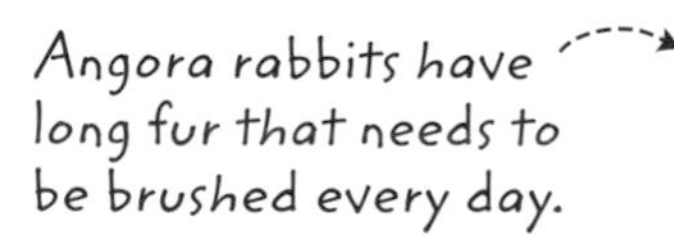

Angora rabbits have long fur that needs to be brushed every day.

Crossbreeds

Baby rabbits look like a mixture of both parents. If the parents are different breeds the babies are called crossbreeds.

Big ears

Some rabbits, called lop-eared rabbits, have big, droopy ears. Their ears can grow so big they touch the ground.

These ears are an average size for a lop-eared rabbit.

Bob tail

A rabbit's tail is called a bob tail. It is short and fluffy, and white underneath. When a rabbit is feeling anxious, it sticks its tail up.

Choosing a rabbit

Baby rabbits can leave their mothers at eight weeks old. You can buy them at this age, or you could adopt adult rabbits from a rescue shelter.

Here are some of the things to look for when choosing a rabbit:

See that its ears are clean.
A healthy rabbit will not be too skinny or fat. Make sure its back feels firm.
Make sure it is breathing quietly and evenly.

Choose a rabbit with bright eyes, glossy fur and a clean, dry nose.

Ask to be shown its teeth. They should be clean and straight.

See that there aren't any cuts, lumps or bald patches.

Where to buy

You can buy rabbits from breeders and pet stores, or you could visit a rescue shelter. Also try asking around – one of your friends might have some baby rabbits that need a home.

Which ones?

Choose the rabbits that look most lively and playful.

Make sure they're healthy, then ask the owner how to pick them up. Give them a stroke to calm them down.

Ask if the rabbits are male or female. Male rabbits are called bucks and females are called does.

Watch out for them scratching. If they do, they may have mites, and need to see a vet.

This rabbit is scratching a lot, so it may have mites.

Two better than one

Pet rabbits get lonely on their own, because in the wild they live in large groups. So buy two rabbits if you can.

A male and female get along best.

Two females get along okay, but two males might fight. A male and a female is your best bet, but make sure they've had an operation so they can't have babies.

What will I need?

Before you bring your rabbit home, make sure you have everything ready. You can buy the things you need from a pet store or online.

Carrying box

You'll need a box to bring your rabbits home. Pet stores sell carrying boxes, or you could just use a strong cardboard box, with at least twelve coin-sized air holes cut in its sides.

Whatever sort of box you use, make sure it has holes in the sides.

Line the carrying box with hay.

Food and drink

Buy a food dish for each rabbit and some food to fill it.

Heavy pottery dishes are good because they don't tip over.

Buy some hay from a store. Make sure there's always fresh hay for your rabbits to eat.

A water bottle keeps their drinking water clean and fresh. Buy one with a metal spout, so your rabbits can't chew on it.

Attach the water bottle to the hutch.
Check the spout's not blocked each day.

Hutches

Pet rabbits live in hutches, unless they're indoor rabbits. Hutches are divided into two – a living area where the rabbits eat, and a warm, safe area where they can hide away and sleep.

A hutch should be at least 1.2m (4ft) long, and high enough for rabbits to stand up inside.
Make sure the roof is waterproof.
Long legs keep the hutch clear of the ground.
The wire doors let in fresh air.

If you leave the hutch outside all year, put it in a sheltered spot away from wind, rain and strong sunlight.

Bedding

Lay some newspaper on the floor of the hutch and cover it with wood shavings. Then leave some hay in the sleeping area so your rabbits can make their bed.

Make sure the hay is clean and dry.

Rabbits are clean animals and tend to leave their droppings in one corner. Put some extra wood shavings down there.

"If you wouldn't mind turning the page..."

Settling in

When you bring your rabbits home, they may be frightened by all the strange new things around them. To help them feel safe, lift them gently into their hutch. Here's how to do it:

Slide one of your hands under the rabbit's chest and raise it up slightly.

Use smooth movements.

Place your other hand under your rabbit's bottom, and lift it up.

Lift your rabbit slowly.

Hold your rabbit to your chest, like this, while still supporting its bottom.

Stay kneeling down so your rabbit doesn't try to jump away.

Place your rabbit bottom-first into its hutch, then leave it for a few hours, to get used to its new home.

Always stroke rabbits in the direction their fur grows.

Making friends

Your rabbits will need to get used to you before you start playing with them. First of all, hold out your hand, so they can learn your smell.

Stretch your hand out very slowly like this.

Your new rabbit will take a careful sniff.

Once your rabbits have got used to your smell, feed them small pieces of food from your hand.

Offering carrots is a good way to make friends.

Now you can start stroking them gently. Once they are used to you touching them, you can lift them out of their hutch.

Remember to take things slowly.

Pairing pets

New rabbits also need to make friends with each other before you can leave them together in their hutch. Put them in their run with plenty of food and toys. If a fight breaks out, separate them and try again later.

Make sure the hutch is big enough for two.

Let them sniff and get to know each other.

Outdoors

Wild rabbits roam around in fields eating lots of fresh grass, so pet rabbits like to graze as well. Let them do it as often as possible, but in a safe place where they can't escape.

Let your rabbits out of their hutch to graze.

You could put out some obstacles for them to explore.

Rabbit runs

Runs are safe places where rabbits can graze. You can attach a run to the front of their hutch – that way your rabbits still have shelter from heat and rain.

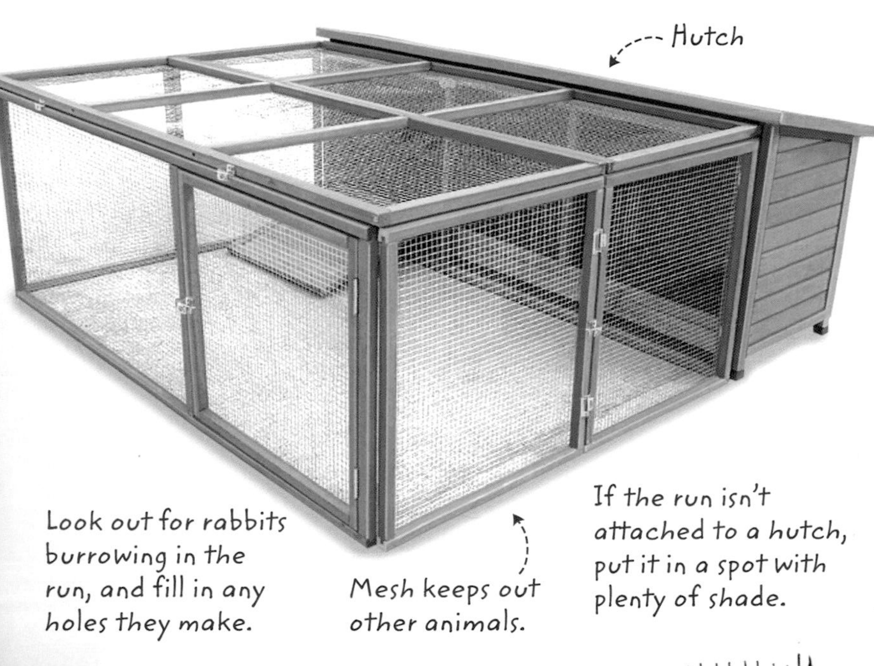

Look out for rabbits burrowing in the run, and fill in any holes they make.

Mesh keeps out other animals.

If the run isn't attached to a hutch, put it in a spot with plenty of shade.

Runs are best put on grass, but if yours is on concrete, make sure you give your rabbits some hay and a box filled with soil to dig in.

A safe spot

Make sure there's no weedkiller on the grass where you put the run. Also watch out for daisies, buttercups and dog or cat waste, which are all poisonous to rabbits.

Setting up the run

Put the run in a place that's sheltered from strong winds, rain and bright sunlight.

Prepare the run for your rabbits.

Although your rabbits will probably have plenty of fresh grass in the run, give them some dry food, hay and water as well.

When everything is ready, lift your rabbits out of their hutch and put them into the run. Then close the door and lock it, so they can't escape.

Don't forget to lock the door.

Make sure each rabbit has a place in the run where it can shelter and hide.

Put hay in the sheltered area.

Rabbit food

Rabbits need a variety of dry food, fresh food and lots of hay. Feed them dry food in the morning and fresh food later on.

Dry food

Pellets are the best dry food, because they have all the vitamins and minerals that rabbits need. If you feed your rabbits pieces of dried fruit and vegetables, they'll only pick out the ones they like best and leave the rest.

MUNCH
MUNCH
Rabbit pellets
Mixed dry food is okay, but pellets are better.

How much?

When your rabbits are young, put plenty of food in their dish each morning. They will eat as much as they need.

Spoon the pellets into a small bowl.

When your rabbits are six months old, only give them a few teaspoons of pellets, or they'll get fat.

Rabbits should finish their pellets in about an hour. The rest of the day is spent grazing on fresh food and hay.

Hay

Hay is dried grass. Rabbits like to munch on hay all through the day, so make sure there's always plenty in your rabbits' hutch.

Put fresh hay in the rack every day.

Treasure hunt

In the wild, rabbits have to search for tasty nibbles, so pet rabbits enjoy doing the same. Try hiding chopped carrots around their run and let your rabbits sniff them out.

You could stuff a plant pot with hay and carrots.

Water

Rabbits need lots of water, especially when the weather is hot. Bowls of water can get dirty in a hutch, so use a water bottle. Remember to fill it with fresh water every day.

Attach the bottle to the side of the hutch, where your rabbits can reach it.

Rabbits drink with quick little sips.

Celery

Fresh food

Your rabbits need to eat fresh vegetables every day to stay fit and healthy.

What to give

They like eating raw vegetables such as carrots, broccoli, cauliflower and celery.

Lettuce is no good, because it gives them an upset stomach. Fruit is okay as an occasional treat.

What not to give

Rabbits should only eat vegetables, fruit, hay and grass. Anything else could be bad for them.

Chocolate can make rabbits ill.

Treats

Too much soft fruit is bad for rabbits, but a few strawberries and raspberries every now and again make an exciting treat.

"Mmmm, delicious!"

How much?

Every day, rabbits should be given a mound of fresh food about half the size of their body.

Preparing fresh food

Wash the vegetables to get rid of any chemicals. Carefully cut them into chunky pieces.

Rabbits like nibbling their food, so make the chunks quite large.

Put fresh food in your rabbits' dishes in the afternoon or early evening.

When you clean out the hutch before bed, take away anything that hasn't been eaten. Food that starts to go bad can make your rabbit very sick.

Mixing it up

Rabbits are fussy eaters and it takes them time to get used to new food. The best way to get them eating something new is to mix it with food they already like.

Mix a few chunks of new vegetables into their usual dinner.

Try adding a couple of radishes.

If they don't touch the new food, you can try a few more times, but don't force it.

Playtime

Rabbits should be let out of their hutch at least once a day, because they like playing and need plenty of exercise. They're most active in the morning and evening, so these times are best.

Let your rabbit play in its run, or any place where it can't escape.

Rabbits enjoy having flower pots to hide in.

Adventure playground

You can make an adventure playground by putting out flower pots, pieces of drainpipe and other things to play with.

Rabbits will crawl through short drainpipes.
Make sure the pipes are wide enough for them to fit through.
Willow balls can be bought from pet stores.

Chewing

Rabbits have very sharp teeth that grow all the time. Wild rabbits keep their teeth short by chewing plants and roots.

If you feed your rabbits the correct diet, their teeth will stay short and healthy, too.

Hay and grass keep a rabbit's teeth short.

Rabbits chew on carrots and other hard vegetables.

Burrowing

Wild rabbits live in burrows, so your pet rabbits might try to dig tunnels when they're out playing.

Rabbits dig with their front feet...
... and kick the soil out of the way with their back feet.

Territory

Rabbits mark the areas where they feel safe with a scent that humans can't smell. These areas are called their territory.

Rabbits have scent glands on their chins.

If they rub their scent on you, they're letting other animals know you're part of their territory.

Handling

The more you handle your rabbits, the tamer they will become. Try stroking their noses – most rabbits like that.

It's best not to pick them up very often, though. Some rabbits get nervous and might struggle and injure themselves.

Handling tips

It's also not a good idea to walk around with a rabbit in your arms. They have a strong kick, and might jump away and hurt themselves.

If your rabbit starts struggling, gently put it back in its hutch.

Stroke your rabbit gently to keep it calm.

If you do pick them up, remember to support them correctly.

Pick your rabbits up like this...

...then hold them to your chest.

Other people might want to pick up one of your rabbits. Make sure they know the correct way to hold it, so it feels safe in their arms.

"Yes, and don't hold him too tight, either."

Habits

It's natural for rabbits to dig and chew things, so give them lots of toys and a digging box.

Rabbits like finding things to chew.

You can buy chew-toys from pet stores.

If they chew on something they shouldn't, don't shout at them or smack them. They'll be scared and won't understand why you're doing it.

Runaway rabbits

When your rabbits are out playing, they may be difficult to catch. Don't chase them, because it just scares them off.

Hold some food in your hand and let them come to you.

Let them eat the food, then pick them up and carry them back to their hutch.

Fur

Fur is what keeps your rabbits warm and dry. Rabbits clean their own fur, but you can help by grooming them too.

Keeping clean

Rabbits spend a lot of time washing and grooming. They use their teeth, tongue and paws to pick out dirt or anything else that's got stuck.

Rabbits use their paws like a brush...

...and their tongue like a cloth.

Giving space

Rabbits like to clean their whole body at once, so leave them to it when they get started. They might also spend time grooming each other.

They twist around to wash their fur...

...and hold their ears to clean them out.

Grooming

Groom your rabbits once a week and their fur should stay clean and healthy. Rabbits groom each other as a way of making friends so they'll probably like being groomed by you.

Sit each one on an old towel, and brush the fur on its back, going from neck to tail.

Then stand it up with your hands around its chest. Rest its back against your knees.

Your rabbit should be nice and relaxed by now.

Gently brush your rabbit's stomach in the direction its fur grows.

You can buy brushes from a pet store or use any soft brush.

Shedding

In spring and autumn, your rabbits may shed more fur than usual. When this happens, groom them each day to get rid of the loose fur.

Long-haired rabbits

Rabbits with long fur need to be groomed every day. Brush the fur, one section at a time, from the roots to the ends. Then do the same with a comb.

Hold each section of fur as you brush it.

Wide-toothed comb

What does it mean?

You can tell how your rabbits are feeling by the way they behave.

On the lookout

When rabbits see or hear something strange, they stand up on their back legs to scan the area. Their ears stand up straight so they can hear every sound.

Your rabbit may stand like this if it feels in danger, or if it sees you bringing food.

"Looks like carrots again, Cecil."

Feeling scared

In the wild, rabbits run away when they're scared. Their tails are white underneath, to signal the danger to other rabbits.

If a rabbit is very scared, it lies completely still, close to the ground and folds its ears back. If your rabbit does this, leave it alone because it's trying not to be seen.

The ears are pressed right down into its back.

Something new

Rabbits give anything new a good sniff, to get used to its smell. In fact, smell is the main way they recognize things.

Rabbits have a keen sense of smell.

No threats

If you see your rabbits stretched out on their front, they're relaxed and feeling safe. If your rabbits want to sleep, they'll shut their eyes and lie on their side with a leg stuck out.

Rabbits sometimes sunbathe like this, too.

Eating droppings

Don't worry if your rabbits eat some of their own droppings. They do it because the droppings have nutrients in them.

Bathtime

You may see your rabbit flicking one of its paws out. This means it's going to start grooming itself.

If your rabbit flicks its paw out, leave it alone to groom.

Cleaning out

Rabbits are clean animals, but you should still clear their run and hutch regularly or they could get sick. Always wash your hands when you've finished, to get rid of any germs.

Every day

Make sure your rabbits have fresh hay to eat. If they have a hay rack, you can use old hay from the rack as new bedding.

Put your rabbits in their run while you clean the hutch.

Rabbits usually leave their droppings in a corner of their living area. Remove them with a plastic spatula or spade.

Rabbits will rub their scent on new bedding.

After you've cleaned the hutch, your rabbit may rearrange the new hay.

Take the dishes and empty out any old food. Then wash them well and dry them with a towel.

Throw away uneaten food at the end of every day.

Every other day

Throw away all wood shavings, newspaper and bedding hay. Use a dustpan and brush to sweep out the hutch.

Scrape the dirt from the corners with a plastic spatula.

Buy special disinfectant from your pet store.

Spray the hutch with pet-safe disinfectant and let it dry.

Lay newspaper on the bottom of the hutch and cover it with fresh wood shavings and hay.

Push a brush into the water bottle and scrub it with clean water. Wash your hands when you've finished.

What you need

These are the things you need. Don't use them to clean anything but your rabbits' hutch.

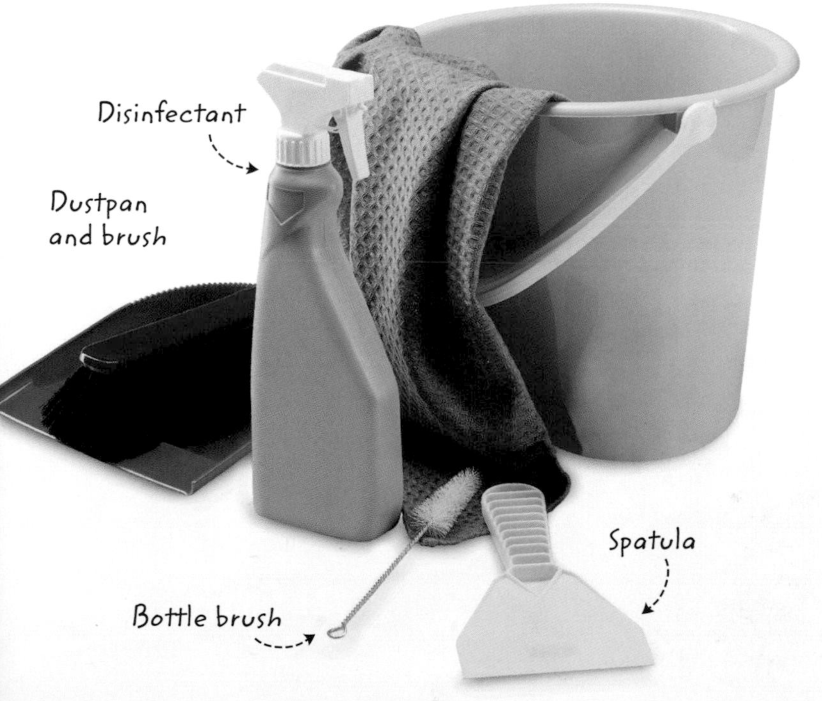

Going to the vet

Even healthy rabbits need to be taken to the vet every now and again. They need an operation to stop them from having babies, and may need vaccinating against diseases.

Getting there

Take your rabbit to the vet in a carrying box. Cover the box with a cloth so your rabbit isn't scared by the other animals in the waiting room.

Make sure the journey is as smooth as possible.

Vets treat all sorts of different animals.

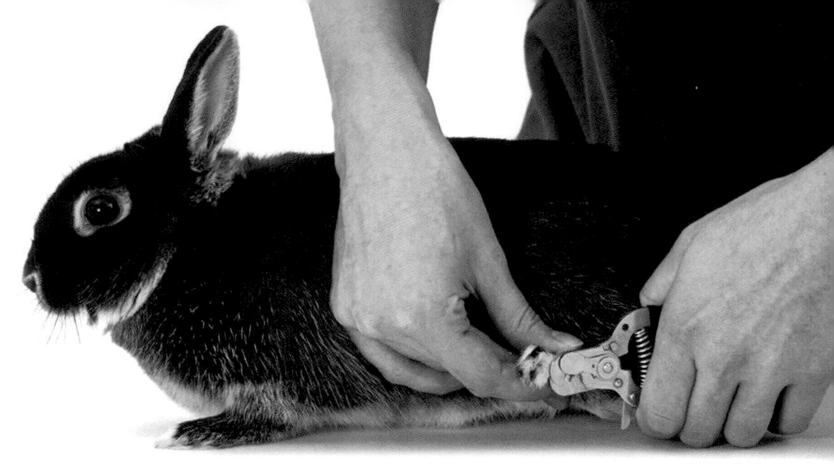

A vet clipping a rabbit's claws

Teeth and claws

When your rabbits' claws grow too long, go to a vet or pet store to get them clipped.

Your rabbit's claws should be 1/2cm (1/4in) long.

If your rabbits' teeth aren't straight, they'll grow too long and stick out at a strange angle. If this happens, ask your vet to shorten them.

Vaccination

If you live in Europe, Australia or New Zealand, your rabbits will need vaccinating every year to prevent nasty diseases.

Fur mites

If you see your rabbit scratching a lot, it may have fur mites. These are little creatures that live in a rabbit's fur and make its skin itch.

Dealing with mites

If you think your rabbit has fur mites, you need to take it to the vet. You shouldn't treat it yourself unless your vet has given you the right powder.

This scratching rabbit may have fur mites.

Put on some old gloves and lift it into a carrying box.

Lift your rabbit gently into the box.
Make sure the carrying box is lined with hay.
Your vet will have a powder for killing fur mites.

Take your rabbit to the vet, who will give it the right treatment.

Staying healthy

If you look after your rabbits properly they'll most likely stay healthy. But check them every day, just to make sure.

If you think one of your rabbits is sick, you must take it to a vet right away. Turn over the page to learn some of the warning signs.

Health checks

Your rabbit may be sick if it has trouble breathing or if it's not eating or drinking much.

It's a bad sign if your rabbit won't eat its food.

Check your rabbit's eyes, nose and ears regularly. If they are runny, it may have the flu.

Check to see if your rabbits are limping or keeping one of their paws off the ground. If they are, they may have an injury.

This rabbit is limping because it's hurt its paw.

Looking after your rabbit

If your rabbits have any of these problems, take them to the vet. Rabbits sometimes hide how sick they are, so their condition could be worse than it looks.

A vet will patch your rabbit up.

Getting older

Most rabbits live for about eight years. As they grow older, they become more sleepy and may need help keeping clean.

This rabbit is nine years old.

Indoor rabbits

You can keep pet rabbits indoors as long as they get plenty of exercise. But first of all you have to make sure your house is safe.

Keep an eye on your rabbits when they're playing outside their cage.

They'll enjoy nosing around together.

Put out old cushions and other things for them to explore.

Rabbits like chewing and digging, so don't leave anything lying around that could be damaged, or be dangerous for them.

Preparations

Indoor rabbits will need a large cage, and a wooden box inside to sleep in.

Put some hay in the wooden box.

Put food and water in the cage, and cover the floor with wood shavings.

Keep your rabbits away from dangers such as hot drinks, people's feet and anything sharp.

Close any doors before you let your rabbits out.

Put cable covers over electric wires, and plug protectors in empty sockets.

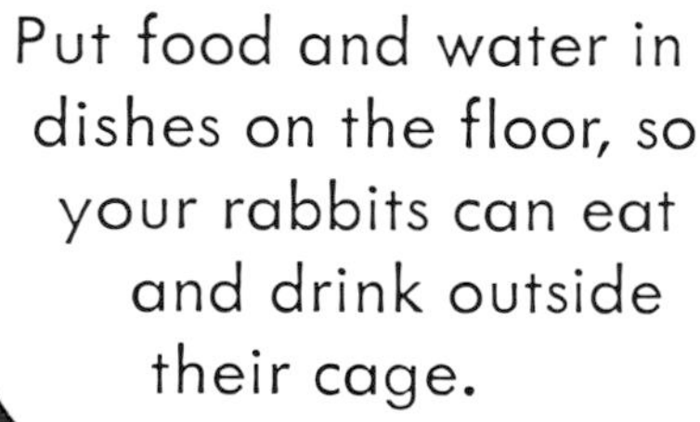

Put food and water in dishes on the floor, so your rabbits can eat and drink outside their cage.

Put the dishes on sheets of newspaper.

Toilet training

If you keep your rabbits indoors, train them to leave their droppings in one place. They're clean animals and usually go in the same spot anyway.

Put a plastic tray down there, and fill it with wood shavings, hay and some old droppings. Your rabbits will soon get the idea and use it by themselves.

Fill a plastic tray with wood shavings and hay.

Put the tray on an old sheet of newspaper.

Cleaning the tray

Empty your rabbit's plastic tray every day. Wash it with warm water and disinfectant every week.

Rabbits don't like a dirty litter tray.

Naughty rabbits

If your rabbits leave droppings outside their tray, wipe a little white vinegar on the spot. They hate the smell so much they'll learn not to go there again.

"Oh I say, is that really necessary?"

Going away

If you go away for a night, make sure you leave your rabbits plenty of hay, food and water. If you're away for longer, take them to a bunny boarding place or ask a friend to look after them.

Carry your rabbits in a carrying box.

This box is made from wicker. Others are made from plastic or cardboard.

Before you go

If a friend agrees to look after your rabbits, they'll have to do all the things you usually do. Write it all down for them.

MORNING
WATER
DRY FOOD
FRESH HAY
EXERCISE
"I thought you said pets were fun!"

If you can't find a friend who's used to looking after rabbits, or if you're away for longer than a week, it's best to take your rabbits to a bunny boarder.

Your vet can point you to somewhere that'll keep them just as clean and safe as you do.

Index

Additional design by Jan McCafferty
Digital manipulation by Keith Furnival

Photo credits

(t-top, m-middle, b-bottom, l-left, r-right)

Cover (l) Petra Wagner/naturepl.com; **Cover (r)** Jane Burton/naturepl.com; 7b, 11m, 41b, 44r, 46b, 47, 53t, 54b, 57t Jane Burton/Warren Photographic; 11tr Lepas/Shutterstock; 19b Istvan Csak/Shutterstock; 20, 34tr Tierfotoagentur/Alamy; 21m Rabbit Shack; 34b, 46m Jiri Vaclavek/Shutterstock; 37r Eric Isselée/Shutterstock; 40mr Four Oaks/Shutterstock

First published in 2013 by Usborne Publishing Ltd, Usborne House, 83-85 Saffron Hill, London EC1N 8RT, England. www.usborne.com

UE. Printed in Dongguan, Guangdong, China.